THE CUTT

THE CUTTING EDGE

Clinging to God in the face of self-harm

Jess Wilson

Authentic

MILTON KEYNES ● COLORADO SPRINGS ● HYDERABAD

First published 2008 by Authentic Media
9 Holdom Avenue, Bletchley, Milton Keynes, Bucks, MK1 1QR, UK
1820 Jet Stream Drive, Colorado Springs, CO 80921, USA
OM Authentic Media, Medchal Road, Jeedimetla Village, Secunderabad 500 055,
A.P., India
www.authenticmedia.co.uk
Authentic Media is a division of IBS-STL U.K., limited by guarantee, with its
Registered Office at Kingstown Broadway, Carlisle, Cumbria CA3 0HA.
Registered in England & Wales No. 1216232. Registered charity 270162.

British Library Cataloguing in Publication Data
A catalogue record for this book is available from the
British Library

ISBN-13: 978-1-85078-773-0

Design by James Kessel for Scratch the Sky Ltd (www.scratchthesky.com)
Print Management by Adare
Printed in Great Britain by J.H. Haynes & Co., Sparkford

I'm in the valley of despair
Where no one in my world seems to care.
Why has this darkness chosen me
To pick the apple from the forbidden tree?
How does a caged bird manage to sing
Throughout all its pain and suffering?
I don't hear this lesson's message, and
I'm falling from the cutting edge.

Dedicated to
Tracy Senchal and Gill James
for all the lessons you've both taught me

CONTENTS

ACKNOWLEDGEMENTS

This book would never have come into existence had it not been for my loving Almighty Father; words cannot express what you've done for me and the debt that I owe you. My life would be purposeless without you.

A massive thank-you to my amazing family and wonderful friends, who have supported me relentlessly through good and bad. Mum, I love you more than anything of this world – thank you for everything.

Nigel and Gary; I am so proud to be a part of Ignite. Thank you so much for all the support, encouragement and opportunities that you have both given me over the last ten years. It's been such a privilege working with you on this project – thank you so much for sharing this vision with me.

Abigail; you are an amazing young woman. God has blessed you with so many gifts and talents. You've been a friend for as long as I can remember. I love you so dearly – you are my sister.

Emma and Sara; I share so many memories, good and bad, with both of you and the relationships that I have with you have been two of the most honest, consistent and valuable. I really do thank God for you.

Anna; your support is staggering. Thank you for your continuous and unrelenting love, encouragement and honesty – even when I didn't want to hear it! You and Peter are both role models to me.

Tracy; thank you for helping me to change my perspectives. You are such an incredibly talented, caring, self-sacrificial and yet unassuming person. You've taught me so much in so many different ways. I'll never forget what you did for me.

Gill; I don't get to see you as much as I'd like to but I love you so dearly. I could never put a price on your support and encouragement. You are such an inspiration to me.

Richard; thank you for allowing me to use your incredibly powerful testimony. You are amazing and God has such an awesome plan for your life. Your story brings me to tears. And to Clare, thank you for allowing me to use your unique testimony as part of this project.

Lastly, my sincere thanks go to Emma Newrick and everyone at Authentic Media who have worked tirelessly on this project; thank you for making my dream become a reality.

WHY I'M WRITING THIS

A few years ago, I discovered that the one thing that I was in need of most – a Christian book on self-harm – was not available. I don't doubt that there are books like this out there; I simply failed to find them. I was lucky enough to find some superb secular books that helped me greatly, but what I really could have done with was a book that could show me God's perspective and could advise and encourage me from a Christian point of view. So I decided to write one.

I wanted to write a book that would primarily help the self-harmer but also their friends and family. I've experienced both ends of the spectrum; I've been the self-harmer so I know how it feels to be unable to see any way out, and I've also wanted to support friends through their self-harming behaviour but felt powerless to do so. I hope this book will provide some of the guidance I was looking for, and that reading it makes a difficult time easier.

> I want to encourage you, the reader, that there is hope and there is most definitely a bright shining light at the end of the tunnel.

I want to encourage you, the reader, that there is hope and there is most definitely a bright shining light at the end of the tunnel, no matter how long and dark the tunnel feels right now. You may have countless friends and family members who are supporting and helping you to get through this time and that is fantastic, but remember that Jesus is also there for you and wants to be with you through these times of trouble. Place your faith in him and your life in his hands

The LORD your God is with you,
he is mighty to save.

He will take great delight in you,
he will quiet you with his love,
he will rejoice over you with singing
(Zeph. 3:17).

Yes, *you!*

WHAT IS SELF-HARM AND WHY DO PEOPLE DO IT?

'Self-harm' is the term used for when someone deliberately causes harm to him or herself. It is not uncommon – in fact, it's the total opposite. Recent studies estimate that self-harm affects between 1 in 12 and 1 in 15 young people who live in the UK.[1] The term covers all types of deliberate injury, ranging from hitting to burning, scratching and poisoning. But the most frequently talked about type of self-harm is cutting.

It is not a new phenomenon either – even in the Bible we hear of self-harm, recounted by Mark in his Gospel (Mk. 5:3–5).

Some shocking yet very important self-harm statistics

Studies have shown that 43 per cent of people who are asked know someone who has self-harmed.[2] During 2004, ChildLine counselled almost four thousand three hundred children and young people about self-harm, the vast majority (91 per cent) of which were girls. The number of young people disclosing self-harm to ChildLine has risen by almost 30 per cent in the last year. The number of calls about self-harm has been rising at an average rate of 23 per cent per year since 1994. The group with the highest rates of self-harm is young women aged fifteen to nineteen years. In all age groups, females are more likely to self-harm than males.[3]

Studies have shown that 43 per cent of people who are asked know someone who has self-harmed.

Self-harm, unlike parasuicide, can also include habitual behaviours such as self-cutting or poisoning, which usually do not have suicidal intent, although there is the risk of accidental death.[4] However, several studies have shown that approximately one out of every hundred people who are seen at hospital for self-harm will die by suicide within a year.[5] This is a suicide risk approximately one hundred times that of the general population.[6]

A national survey of children and adolescents carried out in the community found that 5 per cent of boys and 8 per cent of girls aged thirteen to fifteen said that they had, at some time, tried to harm, hurt or kill themselves. Rates of self-harm reported by parents were much lower than the rates of self-harm reported by children. This suggests that many parents are unaware that their children are self-harming.[7]

Why self-harm?

Because we are all totally unique and different from each other, it is impossible to accurately pinpoint why people self-harm. Just as with addictions and eating disorders, each sufferer has their own individual reasons. Through research such as psychological studies we can gain an insight into some of the causes behind self-harm, but we must understand that self-harmers can be of all ages and come from all walks of life. There is no such thing as a stereotypical self-harmer.

However, modern culture has encouraged the myths and stereotypes surrounding self-harm. For example, it is often assumed that the alternative music scene encourages self-harm, and this reinforces the misconception that it is something that only young people trying to find their identity do. Another stereotype draws on the idea that mental health problems such as schizophrenia are directly related to self-harm. These suggestions are incorrect.[8] Self-harm is something that can affect anyone of any age and background. Each person has reached their own point of desperation and has, for reasons that can be very different, felt the need to self-harm.

> **Self-harm is something that can affect anyone of any age and background.**

Another myth is that all self-harmers are suicidal. It *is* true that some people do end their lives through cutting themselves, but I must stress that suicide is not the intention of the majority of self-harmers. For some, self-harm is a cry for help as they feel that nobody understands what they are going through, and they can find no other way of expressing those feelings other than through cutting themselves. In addition, self-harmers often describe the action of cutting as therapeutic; the loss of blood from their bodies can symbolize the release of an emotional pain.

Each self-harmer will have their own story, their own feelings, views and reasons, just as I did and just as millions of other people have had and will have.

MY STORY

My self-harming began as a coping mechanism for the way I felt about myself. For me, the fear of failure has always been a big problem. I never felt like I was good enough. I set myself incredibly high targets, and continually felt like a failure when I couldn't meet them. I felt that I was letting myself, my family, my friends and also God down in every part of my life.

This really was not due to other people or their actions; my family have never pushed me in any way, my teachers never asked too much of me, my friends and I never competed against each other. It was my own mind that set my targets and standards.

> I was screaming with hate for myself and everything that made me who I was.

I suffered especially from low self-esteem, unbeknown to many of my friends and family. On the outside, I was confident, outgoing and extroverted, but on the inside I was screaming with hate for myself and everything that made me who I was. I was pretty average; I wasn't too fat or too thin, I was relatively popular, I was musically talented (though I didn't think so) and I was loved unconditionally by my family, but these things weren't enough to keep me from loathing myself.

At school, I was a 'model student'. I was liked by both pupils and teachers alike, represented the school in countless competitions, and filled my dinner hours and free time with copious amounts of extra-curricular activities. I was more or less the perfect student; to everyone other than myself that is. I felt that I was useless at everything; even the subjects in which I excelled. French has been and always will be my passion but I can vividly remember telling my teacher that I was going to fail my exam, and begging her to enter me for a lower level paper.

Now, when I say 'fail' what I meant was that I would only get an A and not an A*, and heaven forbid that I should get a B. I even told her that I would rather get an F than a B, as if I got a B everyone would say I'd done well, and no one would understand that as far as I was concerned, I'd failed. Luckily, she did not grant me my wish. Of course, she could see what I couldn't; that I was being totally irrational. I wrote in my diary that day: 'I'm just not being taken seriously – either she [my teacher] can't see that I'm useless or she's just ignoring the fact.' Of course, I wasn't being ignored and my opinions were being taken into consideration.

My teacher knew what she was talking about. I simply refused to believe her. I would set myself unrealistic goals and then hate myself when I didn't reach them: if I didn't get 100 per cent in certain tests; if I wasn't always top of my class; if I made a mistake with pronunciation, I was a failure. And as for exam periods . . . my teachers deserve awards for putting up with me.

As much as they may have felt I was simply being dramatic, I was truly petrified of 'failing'. Exam time brought anxiety, waterfalls of tears and panic attacks. I was comforted countless times, given mugs of calming fruit tea, and encouraged relentlessly, for which I will be eternally grateful. But sadly, when I received my incredibly high GCSE results I felt that, although they were amongst the best in my year, they still weren't good enough, and therefore, I wasn't good enough either.

Self-harm for me was a mixture of self-punishment and release.

Self-harm for me was a mixture of self-punishment and release. Naturally, a vicious circle quickly began: I set a standard, I didn't meet it, I felt like a failure, I cut myself, I felt like a failure for cutting myself, so I cut myself . . . To anyone else, and to me now looking back on it, that sounds completely irrational. At the time, though, it seemed logical. Sure, I was harming myself, but how do others deal with their feelings of failure? I had friends who drank; I had friends who'd had eating disorders; those who smoked – what's the big deal with self-harm? Another irrational idea of mine.

> Self-harm didn't solve any of my problems; in fact it only made them worse.

I self-harmed for nearly two years before I told anyone who could help me in ways that my friends couldn't. I never did it to seek attention; in fact it was quite the opposite. To be honest, I didn't want to tell anyone. I knew that I was becoming addicted, but by now self-harming was my coping mechanism. The need to self-harm would take over my mind when I was feeling desperate. The physical pain somehow seemed to lessen my emotional pain. But after the initial release, within a couple of hours, the pain and self-hate would rise up within me again. Self-harm didn't solve any of my problems; in fact it only made them worse. It actually became less of a coping mechanism and more of a problem in its own right. At one point, I was even self-harming to punish myself for previous self-harm. My close friends threatened to tell someone if I didn't do so myself; I'm so thankful that they saw the severity of the situation and did something about it. Telling one of my teachers was the most difficult and yet most liberating thing I have ever done. Afterwards, I wrote: 'I spent the whole of first lesson totally scared about what she'd say and how she'd react, and was having major panic moments and feeling really sick although I hadn't eaten in nearly a day; *but* although I felt really stupid having to go through everything with her and explaining all the how's and why's, she was so lovely with me . . . and just made me feel better and understood. She was just so supportive.' I was soon on the road to recovery.

Recovery doesn't just happen in an instant, though; it's a long process, but always worth it. And yes, I slipped up, but I got back up again with the help of God and my friends. I went for eight months before I self-harmed again, and when I did I felt such a failure. That is, until I was reminded that eight months without self-harming is not a failure; it's a long time and perhaps next time I could go for longer. It was then I decided to see a doctor. This was another very hard step to take but an incredible beneficial and freeing one. The same teacher then organized for me to see someone in school – there was no end to her commitment.

In the end, I got through my A-levels without any problems. Of course, there were tears as usual but no cutting, which was amazing. I had cut my way through eight sets of exams, but for the first time I got through them without even an urge to release my emotions and anxieties in that way. I left my secondary school feeling that whereas some people would be remembered as very good students, I would always be remembered as the one who did well considering her 'problems'. I now know this to be untrue! It is now well over two years since my last urge, let alone my last cut.

You may be wondering where God was while I was going through all of this.

You may be wondering where God was while I was going through all of this. Had I said anything to God during this time, it would have been: 'Where are you?' In all honesty, at times I didn't feel him near at all. Looking back though, he was continually there, working in me. I was simply choosing not to see him. He was in the comforting words of my friends, the reassuring words of my teachers, in the songs that I was listening to. So many people were praying for me and their prayers were answered. My cries of desperation were heard. Had I possessed a little more faith, or had I bothered to listen to him, then maybe my road would not have been so long and hard. But I don't look at my scars and feel ashamed and I don't hate myself for what I did. When I see my scars, they remind me of what God has brought me through and what he did for me. He can do that for you, too.

I'M A CHRISTIAN, SO WHY IS THIS HAPPENING TO ME?

If you make the Most High your dwelling –
Even the LORD, who is my refuge –
then no harm will befall you,
no disaster will come near your tent.
For he will command his angels concerning you
to guard you in all your ways;
they will lift you up in their hands,
so that you will not strike your foot against a stone
(Ps. 91:9–12).

Often people think that becoming a Christian means that we'll somehow be protected from pain and sadness. And reading this psalm seems to confirm that. But, of course, we do get hurt. So what does this psalm mean?

Psalm 91 encourages us, God's people, to live by faith and not by fear. He promises to protect his people if they trust in him. And it's not just the psalmist who speaks; in verses 14–16, God himself speaks. But why do Christians suffer? Why doesn't God deliver his people from harm? What good is a promise that doesn't seem to be kept? *What* is promised and *how* is it kept?

We see that God doesn't promise his people that there won't be trouble.

In actual fact, if we study the psalm closely, we see that God doesn't promise his people that there won't be trouble. What he states is that he'll go through the trials with them and that they will be ultimately delivered from them. God's people won't be touched by the rebellious acts that are committed against them. God won't punish his own people. They will see the rebellious judged, but they won't be judged as well – God's people will come through it.

It is vital that we know our Bibles well so that we know what the promises of God actually are. And God *has* kept his promise; by raising his one and only Son, Jesus, from the dead. It was this psalm that Satan misquoted to Jesus when he was tempted in the desert. We often read the Bible and are so quick to say 'It's me!' but we must understand that the Bible is more than that: it is a revelation of God himself. This psalm is pointing to more hope in the New Testament – a lasting hope, an everlasting hope, the hope of eternal life.

God has promised to protect us if we trust in Jesus. He will do for us what he has done for his Son. We won't be judged as rebels on the last day. We have the hope of verse 13 to hold on to

You will tread upon the lion and the cobra;
you will trample the great lion and the serpent.

We could relate verse 13 to how we feel and to our self-harming behaviour. God will be with us and will help us to trample the serpent and lion (the self-harm in our case) if we let him. And we know that he will follow through, because of the promise that he has made to us, through Jesus.

SELF-IMAGE AND THE MEDIA

Below are two passages that specifically talk about self-image from God's perspective

> *Oh yes, you shaped me first inside, and then out; you formed me in my mother's womb . . . Body and soul I am marvelously made . . . you know every bone in my body; you know exactly how I was made, bit by bit, how I was sculpted from nothing into something. Like an open book, you watched me grow from conception to birth; all the stages of my life were spread out before you (Ps. 139:13–16, The Message).*

> *The LORD does not look at the things man looks at. Man looks at the outward appearance, but the LORD looks at the heart (1 Sam. 16:7).*

Of all the things that today's world throws at us, insecurity about our self-image is perhaps the most difficult to deal with. To have the perfect hair, figure and looks is totally unachievable, unless you have a personal stylist and make-up artist to work on you for three hours before you go out of the house every morning – which, let's face it, doesn't happen anywhere but Hollywood.

Advertising persistently shouts at us that we must look a certain way to be loved and accepted by society.

Living in the world is hard. The media continually pushes perfection: magazine covers show images of girls whose figures are sizes we didn't even know existed, and their pages are stuffed with advice on what to wear, how to wear it and when to wear it. Advertising persistently shouts at us that we must look a certain way to be loved and accepted by society. The important thing to do when faced with this pressure to look a certain way is to keep a grip on reality.

When you are constantly bombarded with images of tall, thin, beautiful models and tanned and toned A-list stars, it is easy to think 'I should look like that.' But the truth is that you *shouldn't*. You should look exactly as you do. The people in the magazines aren't real, they have been airbrushed, and obviously that's *after* the pictures have been taken. Hours and hours have been put in before the photo shoot to make sure that the person you see in the magazine looks amazing. In reality, you don't have time to spend hours each day making yourself look 'perfect', and you shouldn't feel that you have to. The truth is that if you start looking to God for how you should be instead of at fashion and beauty magazines you will know what it is to be truly beautiful.

No matter how unworthy you feel, God loves you.

I know that it's difficult to trust what God thinks over what the media is telling you. I know what it's like to hate everything about yourself and to wish every part of you was different in one way or another. I also know how it feels to read positive passages in the Bible and feel unworthy to come before God. When you look in the mirror and think 'urgh', all God sees is beauty – as hard as that is for you to imagine. It's not about how you look with God. Your body is simply a shell housing your heart and soul. He loves *you*, the person, and that is not dependent on anything. No matter how unworthy you feel, God loves you enough that he's written how much you mean to him in the best-selling book of all time: the Bible. And that is such an overwhelming idea – to think that you have thrilled the heart of God so much that he wants to tell the whole world about it. Read what is written in Song of Songs, which I have adapted here

How beautiful you are my darling! Oh you are beautiful! My darling, everything about you is beautiful, and there is nothing at all wrong with you. My darling is like a lily among thorns! You have thrilled my heart with one glance of your eyes. How beautiful you are.

All the people who have ever lived are unique and beautiful in God's eyes. He made each and every one; there will never be anyone else who is like you. In Genesis it is written that God made the world and that he saw it was good; God loves everyone exactly as they are. He doesn't think that you need to be fatter or thinner, taller or shorter, change our hairstyle, clothes or wear more make-up.

It is so hard to accept that God thinks that you are an amazing being when inside you hate yourself, and that feeling is not just going to go away. You don't wake up one day loving yourself. It's a long, and sometimes hard, process.

However, with God's help it is possible to learn to love yourself.

However, with God's help it is possible to learn to love yourself and see yourself in the way that God sees you – through his eyes. If you are struggling to see yourself this way, be encouraged that it does get better. But you do need to ask God for his help. Try getting someone you trust to pray with you. You don't even have to give them details of the circumstances; just let them ask God to bless your situation. It may seem simple, but this can be the first step towards loving yourself.

It is so important to remember that God is there *for you*, not just 'there'. He's not there to criticize, pull you down or catch you out. He's there because he loves you, wants to look after you and to have that special relationship with you. He will never tell you that your bum looks big, or that

you need to put a bit more make-up on; it's just not what
he does.

Clare is another girl who found it really hard dealing
with self-image as she was growing up.

Clare's Story

'God saw all that he had made, and it was very good'
(Gen. 1:31). So why do I feel so inadequate?

When I was about fifteen years old, I was so 'together'; I
had the perfect life. Or so everyone thought. On the
outside, I was a clever girl who was popular, had all the
right clothes, a loving boyfriend, and who was given
everything by her parents. But on the inside, I felt like a
fraud. People thought I was clever, while I felt like any
minute I'd crack under the pressure of school work. People
thought I was popular, yet I felt like a misfit who was
different from all her friends. People thought I was an
accomplished musician, but all I could do was compare
myself to others who were far better than me. But by far
the worst part of my self-esteem issue was my appearance.
I had no self-confidence, but I didn't feel I could talk to
anyone about it. I thought that they'd think I was attention-
seeking or fishing for compliments.

People thought I was popular, yet I felt like a misfit.

At the time, I had a boyfriend who was always telling me
how pretty and lovely I was, but I genuinely believed that
the only reason he was saying these things was because he
didn't want to admit to himself that he had an ugly
girlfriend. Although my Christian friends were never
nasty about the way I looked, my best friend at the time
was always making 'jokes' about how big my bum was.
Every time a joke was made, I felt like someone was

chiselling away a chip of my confidence and, although I never let on, it hurt.

I had a big issue with my weight and shape. I am now and was then 5'6", a size 12, and around ten and a half stone. Pretty average, most people would think. Not in my eyes. All I could see around me were people who were taller and slimmer, or shorter and more petite, with bigger breasts, longer legs, better hair, and prettier faces. I used to eat chocolate and crisps, knowing that they'd make me feel better, while all the while they were just fuelling the weight issue. But, however bad I felt about my weight and shape, it was the pretty faces that made me most insecure.

When I got one spot, people would notice and comment on it.

I had quite bad eczema on my face, which would make patches of it red when I got cold. I had auburn hair with a lot of ginger in it, which people would tease me about (in a friendly way, but I took it harshly at the time). When I got one spot, people would notice and comment on it. I felt so ugly I used to avoid eye contact, even with the people I knew best. I hated the thought of looking in the mirror, afraid that my make-up would be smudged, or that my hair would have fallen out of place, and knowing that I would hate what I saw. But still I found myself carrying a mirror with me at all times; I was obsessed with looking in it, just to make sure. The people around me thought I was vain, but they couldn't have been further from the truth. I was so obsessed with my little mirror that I used to look at it in lessons, sneaking it out of my bag or pencil case just to have a glance.

After feeling down and worthless for so long, I went to a Christian Ignite event called 'Igniting a Passion for the Prodigals'. The talk was about God accepting you, even if you've gone away from him, and during the response time, Nigel James (the speaker), asked if anyone who felt like

God wouldn't accept them would come and be prayed for, to know that he was welcoming them with open arms. I'd been a Christian for a few years at this point, and never been away from God for a significant period of time, so I didn't know why what Nigel was saying touched me so much. It was then that I realized that I knew God accepted me, but that I couldn't accept myself. I knew that the only way I'd learn to accept myself was to go and be prayed for, and trust that God would help me like myself again.

> **I burst out crying as I told her how much I hated myself.**

So I walked to the front of the room, and asked a very wise lady who I knew and trusted to pray for me. I burst out crying as I told her how much I hated myself, as I was so overwhelmed by finally being able to tell someone the truth about my life. She prayed that I'd see myself as God saw me, and although I didn't fully understand what she meant at the time, I realized that God didn't see me as I saw myself. She gave me a portion of the Bible (Psalm 139) to read, and explained that God had created me in his own image, and so on the outside, I was exactly how he wanted me to be.

Some people have stories of when, in a split second, or overnight, their situation is changed. Although I do believe that God works like this sometimes, it wasn't the way that my life was changed. She asked me to read Psalm 139 every day and, although I did, for quite a while I just couldn't believe what was written. But through lots of different ways, God gave me more and more verses to back up what she had told me: that to him, I was (and still am) beautiful.

Bit by bit, I did begin to believe what was written in those verses. They have helped me so much, and although I don't wake up every morning, look in the mirror and say

'Wow, I'm stunning!' I do know that to the most important person in my life, I am his creation, and he thinks I'm gorgeous. Sometimes I do still compare myself to other people, but then I remember that I am different to them, only now I know that it's because I'm unique, not because I'm a misfit. Of course there are some days when I don't feel pretty, but it's never depressing or obsessive like it used to be.

I am his creation, and he thinks I'm gorgeous.

I just want to explain a few of the verses that have helped me deal with my self-image and self-esteem issues, because the truth of what God sees in you is too special to be kept a secret!

- Song of Songs 4:7 – 'All beautiful you are, my darling; there is no flaw in you.' The whole book of Song of Songs is a guy talking to a girl, but it's like a picture of God talking to his daughters. When he looks at us, he doesn't think 'a little bit more concealer wouldn't go amiss'. He thinks 'wow – she's amazing!' In God's eyes, we're perfect in every part, because we look like he wants us to look. He created every part of us, as Psalm 139:13 says 'you knit me together in my mother's womb'. God created us. Would he create anything that was less than perfect?

- Song of Songs 4:9 – 'you have stolen my heart with one glance of your eyes'. When God even just catches our eye, our beauty overcomes him. Only he doesn't feel butterflies in his stomach! What he feels when he sees our beauty goes far deeper than that. When he catches our eye, he feels a rush of love for us; he is totally in love with us.

- Isaiah 62:4 – 'You will be called Hephzibah (my delight is in her)'. God says that he is delighted in you because you are his creation. He made us all individuals; we are all unique. So you might wish you looked like someone else, but if we all looked the same life would be really boring. We need to ask God to help us accept ourselves and to see us as he sees us, not as some people want us to see ourselves. We need to look at ourselves not as 'C+, could try harder', but as 'A*, 100 per cent', because God thinks we're beautiful, and that there's no way we could improve our appearance, no matter what we look like.

SPIRITUAL CLEANSING

We cleanse because it purifies our skin. Cleansing removes the grease and the pollution and gets rid of the dirt, making us clean again. Just a few sweeping motions and everything that was there is gone forever. Many of us wouldn't dream of *not* washing our face and body. Would you wake up from a night's sleep and leave the house without washing your face? No. How odd then that so many of us avoid spiritual cleansing, hoping all the dirt will just disappear by itself.

So what is spiritual cleansing? Some deep, profound ritual? No. It simply means coming before God to say sorry and to receive forgiveness. Sin is the barrier between God and us, and we need to tackle our barriers so that we can deepen our relationship with him.

Sin is the barrier between God and us.

I can't underestimate how important this has been for me. Had it not been for God's continuous cleansing and replenishment in my life, my situation would be very different. Being cleansed by God simply means that all the dirt, the sin, the things we have done wrong, are gone forever. God does not record your sin. But it doesn't stop there. He not only takes away all the bad stuff, but he then fills us with goodness – with promises from the Bible, his Holy Spirit, being able to be free from our past . . . the list really does go on and on.

Recently, I've become quite lazy. I'm so tired at the end of the day that I simply take out my contact lenses and go to bed without removing any of my eye make-up. I'm sure you can imagine what I look like in the morning; my face covered in smeared black make-up. Well, just as waterproof mascara can only be fully removed by using make-up remover, sin can only be washed away and forgiven by God. We can only get so far without God's help. Of course, it is important to ask other people for forgiveness so that we can move on in our relationships with them, and knowing that you need to forgive or be forgiven for something is an unpleasant feeling. But other people's forgiveness can't remove our sin. Only God can do that.

But other people's forgiveness can't remove our sin. Only God can do that.

It's so easy to forget that it's not all about God sitting on a cloud thinking 'I'll make them beg and plead and maybe then I'll think about forgiving them!' Luckily for us, that's not how it works. Jesus died for all of our sins so that we could be forgiven. Why then do we find it so hard to make time for Jesus in our day? I am constantly moving my schedule around just to make room for a coffee or dinner or catch up with my friends, regardless of how busy or tired I am. I love socializing, and I'm very committed to my friends; I'm interested to find out how they are, and being with them helps me to relax. I'm always ready to rearrange things to meet a friend, so why aren't I that committed to God?

Why do we find it so hard to come before God and simply say 'I'm sorry'? If I feel I have a problem with a friend, I'm desperate to sort it out as soon as possible. I'll give them a call or we'll meet up, and I can't feel content again until I know that things are back to normal between us. I'm not quite like that with God. I seem to put him on a backburner. I always mean to come back to him but then something 'more important' comes up and there he is, placed back on the shelf again. But honestly, what could be more important than the status of our relationship with our creator? I have often wondered why we dread repentance and keep putting some time out with God off.

At the end of the day, it is simply about us approaching our loving heavenly Father with confidence and asking for that cleansing and replenishment that we all so desperately need. I know that I build it up until it's a massive chore that I then dread doing. But is it ever as bad as we think it will be? No. And isn't it a fabulous feeling after you've sorted things out? Sure, of course it is. Whereas our friends may hold a grudge for a while, God always forgives us and will *never* turn his back on us.

RESTORING YOUR FIRST LOVE

Forsaken

'But I have this against you: you have left the love you had in the beginning. So remember where you were before you fell. Change your hearts and do what you did at first.' (Rev. 2:4–5, Youth Bible)

Lord, those seconds, minutes, hours, days, months and years of intimacy,
And those of overwhelming passion.
Those memories and moments I thought I would cherish forever
But my first love I have forsaken.

Those feelings that only You could see within me
And those words I spoke only to You above.
And those moments of love and closeness
But now I've forsaken my first love.

Oh, I never really lost that relationship
But the opportunities for intimacy just passed me by.
My priorities were changed and I pulled out of Your fast lane,
But now forsaken my first love have I.

I didn't make a point of changing how I was living,
I carried on believing and had faith in my Father above.
I carried on witnessing and spreading Your word
But I was forsaking my first love.

My life became pointless, I was falling apart,
I cried bitter tears at the foot of Your cross.
But the open arms and the beckoning hands I ignored,
I was forsaking my first love – and that first love I lost.

You took me to the quiet place and there you held me dear
You walked with me and talked with me and we laid my sins to
rest.
You put in the hole my guilt had been – Your peace, Your grace,
Your love.
My first love, Lord, I love You, by You I have been so blessed.

If you are a Christian, do you remember the day you gave
your life to Christ? Do you remember how you felt? When
was the last time you felt like that? Yesterday? Last week?
Last year? It's so easy to suddenly go from all to nothing.

If you are a Christian, do you remember the day you gave your life to Christ?

Some people describe that holy moment of coming to know
Jesus for the first time as 'a mountain-top experience',
meaning that it's so full of awe and clarity. Although it's
good to have these kinds of experiences with God, it's not
the only time that God is with us. Think of it this way: from
the top of most mountains is an amazing view. But how
many things grow on those mountain-tops? It's only when
you get further down the mountain and into the valleys that
you see all the flowers, the wildlife, the trees and the fertile
soil. When we are in the valley of our faith, we think that
God is not there, that we have nothing left. In fact, the
opposite is true. We may be in the valley of our faith,
wishing for another mountain-top experience, but God can
see us in that place of fertile ground, where he can plant
things in us to help us grow in our faith.

We make so much of an effort to maintain the
friendships we've established with our peers and
colleagues, and yet so often we forget about maintaining
the most important relationship of all – our relationship
with our heavenly Father. Maybe you've never
experienced the love of Jesus. Perhaps this is something

you would like to consider? Is a relationship with Jesus something that you would love to have?

> **So often we forget about maintaining the most important relationship of all – our relationship with our heavenly Father.**

During my life I've lost so many friendships due to not working at them, and not bothering to keep in touch. Often we expect the other person to make all of the effort and then we ask ourselves why we haven't seen that friend in over a year. It's no different with God, in fact maybe it's even easier to let our relationship with him slip away, as he seems to be easier to ignore.

How often do we blame God for the way our lives seem so messed up and problematic? But if we took a step back and took a long hard look at the situation, would we be able to say that God was in actual fact at the centre of our lives and beings? Even if the answer to that question is no, there is good news. Unlike our friends, no matter how badly we've treated God, no matter how long we've ignored him, or how much we've abused and disobeyed him, he doesn't go off and find new people to hang around with. He's right there, just waiting for us to say sorry so that he can be part of our life again.

Every day I'm realizing how much my relationship with God needs to be worked at. That's the thing though: you do have to work at it. I used to think it would just happen . . . and then I realized that there wouldn't be flashing lights and angels bringing me his messages. I realized that if I wanted to have a relationship with my creator then it wasn't going to be handed to me on a plate. I would have to be sacrificial with certain parts of my worldly life and I would have to give things up in order to deepen my relationship with him.

Many people think that God speaks to us with a big booming voice . . . and sometimes he might do, but often he speaks to us through a passage in the Bible, or when we're praying . . . meaning that we have to actually read the Bible and pray in the first place. That might mean that we have to catch our favourite television show on E4+1 so we can pray when it's on E4, but God totally appreciates every second we spend with him. We're human and God doesn't expect us to be perfect. He knows that we'll make mistakes – it's inevitable. But there's a big difference between trying to change and live for God's glory, and living how we like because 'God loves us anyway'.

God totally appreciates every second we spend with him.

We need to engage with God in order to maintain our relationship with him. God made us unique and loves us unconditionally. Just like our family and friends, God wants us to tell him about what's happening in our lives, the good things as well as the bad. At times of desperation one of the first things we think of doing is to pray to God for a miracle, but when everything is going to plan in our lives – when we pass those exams, find our perfect partner or land our dream job – we forget about him and put him to one side until the next time we are desperate and in need of his guidance and comfort. We cannot expect to have a relationship with him unless we put in the time, just as we would with any other person. It takes work and it takes time, but have you ever noticed how life often seems easier and happier when you are sharing it all with God?

We need to rekindle that passion and relight our fire with God. In a world that is busy 24 hours a day, seven days a week, we need to take time out and just spend some quality one-to-one time with our loving Father. He wants that more than we could ever imagine.

SOME IDEAS FOR QUIET TIME

Even Jesus needed some time alone with his Father – so where does that leave us?

> But Jesus often withdrew to lonely places and prayed (Lk. 5:16).
>
> Be still and know that I am God (Ps. 46:10).

So turn off the television, disconnect your internet, put your phone away, and be still before the King. Find somewhere comfortable where you won't be disturbed.

Be comfortable, but not too comfortable!

We can come before God at any time and in any place, but it's a good idea to set some time apart on purpose and spend it with God. So get yourself comfortable, but not so comfortable that you fall asleep! Sometimes your body can help you draw closer to him

- holding your hands out
- kneeling
- standing
- lying

It's totally up to you.

Take time to be quiet and still

We are so busy with our everyday lives that often we don't make time to just be still in his presence. Be still before your Father. Ask him to help your heart and mind to be still and to get rid of anything that may prevent you from listening to him.

Relax!

Get rid of any tension that is in your body. Relax your muscles and be open to what God has for you. Some people find that meditative music helps their focus and relaxation. Try some worship music, classical music or your own favourite relaxing music. Ask God to pour his peace into you.

Visualize Jesus

Of course, it is far easier to talk to someone and to listen to them when you can see them standing right in front of you. So visualize Jesus sitting beside you or standing before you and keep saying his name over and over again to remind yourself of your focus. Maybe using a focal point would be helpful? Why not try pictures, crosses, or candles? Try using a mental image, for example: resting in God's arms or sitting at his feet.

Read scripture

- Try reading slowly and carefully through a piece of scripture. Stop at any words or phrases that particularly jump out at you. Meditate on these words and phrases, allowing the Holy Spirit to lead your thoughts.
- Imagine yourself in a particular Bible story – use all of your senses (What do you feel? What can you smell?).
- Read the Lord's Prayer and start to slowly meditate on it and its meaning.
- Read chapters four and five of Revelation and come before God's throne.

• Try using other literature, such as the poem *Footprints* (which can be easily found by typing 'Footprints' into any search engine on the internet) and imagine being carried by God.

Keep it simple

Talking to God need not be any different from talking to anyone else. We don't need to put on a front or use big words. Try using one simple phrase: 'Lord Jesus, I love you', 'Father, please heal me' and keep repeating it.

Go walking with Jesus

Go for a walk and look at everything through the eyes of Jesus. Smell what he smells, see what he sees, feel what he feels.

Afterwards, take a few minutes to just sit quietly before carrying on with the busyness of your day, and ask God to show you how you can look at everything you have seen and learnt in your time with him, and how you can apply it to your daily life.

MAKING A DATE WITH JESUS

Maybe imagining Jesus as your lover sounds incredibly strange to you, and it *is* an extraordinary thing to say – that is until you really think about it. Read what it says in Song of Songs 2:8

> *I hear my lover's voice. Here he comes leaping across the mountains . . . (Youth Bible).*

Song of Songs is a poem about how love was supposed to be. Many people are shocked to find a love song in the Bible, yet alone one with explicit lyrics. It shows no embarrassment or awkwardness about love being enjoyed in the way in which it was created to be. If you were to turn on the TV or the radio, what would you hear? Love song after love song. Love is constantly talked about and discussed, so we shouldn't be so surprised when we find this in the Bible, as it was God who first created the thing called 'love'.

If God created love, why does making a date with him seem so bizarre?

If God created love, why does making a date with him seem so bizarre? Is it because the word 'love' has been so badly tainted over the years that we now question what it actually means?

Although human love can be a very beautiful thing, it can come with its conditions. Conditions such as: if you love me I'll do this, or if you loved me you'd do that for me, and so on. As human beings we are selfish, self-centred creatures and even the least selfish of us is incapable of pure unconditional love. God's love, on the other hand, is a very different love. God's love is a pure love, an unadulterated love, an unconditional love – it is anything but human.

You are perfect to him; he simply wants you to get to know him!

If you choose him to be, Jesus can be like an intimate lover that never goes away, never lets you down, never cancels on you or dumps you. He is someone who will not push your boundaries or lead you astray. He won't force anything upon you or put you in compromising positions. Sometimes people can get lonely if they don't have a boyfriend or a girlfriend. They can feel left out, unloved and as though nobody wants them. Let me tell you this – Jesus would jump at the chance of being able to look after you if only you gave him half a chance. He'll never drop you because a better offer has come along, or swap you for a younger/older/prettier/thinner/taller model. You are perfect to him; he simply wants you to get to know him! So why not make a date with him? It only takes three simple steps

Put it in your diary

You wouldn't want to forget, would you? Write a date and time in your diary and set it aside for some personal time with your creator. He won't cancel on you, so don't you cancel on him.

Preparation

Would you dream of going on a date with unwashed hair, an unmade-up face and filthy clothes? Of course not! Well, the same applies to Jesus. You need to prepare your heart and mind for your time together. That means getting rid of anything that might come between you and God. And why not make the effort to get ready as if it were a date with a girlfriend or boyfriend? That way it'll feel like a far more significant moment.

Get excited!

I'm sure I'm not the only person who gets stupidly excited on the way to a date. Go with an open mind and an open heart. Be excited that you are going to have an amazing time with the person who loves you the most – your heavenly Father. And enjoy yourself! Your life is busy 99 per cent of the time, so relax in his presence and count yourself lucky to be spending some precious, quality time with the Almighty One.

PRAISING GOD THROUGH OUR CIRCUMSTANCES

Many people talk about 'praising God through our circumstances', which means praising God in everything that we do, even during the tough times when we feel him to be so far away. It's something that I've always had trouble understanding. Personally, I find it incredibly easy to thank God when things are going really well in my life – if I've passed a hard exam, I've met someone great or I've received some good news. As a general rule I'm easily able to see God working in my life when things are going the right way. But when things happen in my life that I can't fix, that are beyond my control, which upset me and cause me pain, I find it very hard to praise God. Why would I feel like praising God when my life seems to be falling apart around me? I used to think 'What a stupid thing to do! Surely if you can manage to praise God, then the situation you're in can't be that bad.' But I recently had an experience that made me change my mind.

> **Why would I feel like praising God when my life seems to be falling apart around me?**

At the moment, I'm a student at university and living in a huge city during my term times. I've been blessed with an amazing set of friends and barely a week goes by without my visiting one of them or someone coming to stay with me. Some time ago, one of my closest friends came to spend some time with me. Having been great friends from childhood we are very close, and she'd stayed with me plenty of times before. Sadly, this time was different. While she was staying with me, she was raped.

I was not with her at the time, and was horrified when I found out what had happened. I felt a mixture of anger, pain, fear and powerlessness. But the overriding feeling was the familiar one of failure and guilt. All I could think of was 'what if'. What if I had been there, if she hadn't gone, if I had tried harder to persuade her not to meet him or refused to let her go, and above all, if she'd never come to see me. Although I wasn't the one who had subjected her to this ordeal, I still felt that it was somehow my fault.

I felt continually angry because she is someone I love very much, and I hate the thought of someone doing that to anyone, let alone one of my closest friends. I spoke about my feelings of anger and of responsibility to so many different people. People listened to me, supported me, advised me and prayed with me. I even spoke to a prayer counsellor about it, but nothing seemed to make even the slight bit of difference to the way I felt.

People listened to me, supported me, advised me and prayed with me.

Before this happened, I had been at a big Christian conference called Spring Harvest with friends. As one of the evening meetings came to a close, the worship leader finished it with a few worship songs. Another of my friends had been telling me for a long time about a song that had totally changed her outlook on life but I had never heard it until now. That song ('When the Tears Fall' by Tim Hughes) was played that night and it brought me to my knees before God because the words were just so apt for the way I was feeling at that time. I loved it so much that I bought it on iTunes and continually had it on repeat on my iPod.

Wept for my friend and what had happened to her, wept because of the anger I still felt.

A few months later, I found myself in floods of tears, sitting in the kitchen of my university accommodation in the dark, just staring out into the city. This was the city I had initially loved, but now, because of my friend's rape, had become a city I detested and was afraid to be in. I hated the fact that I was potentially sharing a city with a man who'd stolen something so precious from my close friend that she couldn't get it back. It made me feel sick to just be there. I sat in the dark staring at the city whose lights I had loved looking at, and the song came on to my iPod. I listened to it and wept. Wept for my friend and what had happened to her, wept because of the anger I still felt, wept because of the failure and guilt I had burdened myself with, and because of the love I had lost for my life in that city. I realized that although nothing would ever take away the cold hard fact that my friend had been raped there, I was not willing to give her attacker control over my feelings and actions as well as hers. I wouldn't let him make me hate the city I had chosen to be in. It was at that moment that I felt I understood what it meant to praise God through our circumstances. Although I was hurting and my friend was hurting, I remembered that God is God, regardless of any of us and what we are going through. God is God and I could praise him simply for that. I could praise him because I know my friend will be a stronger person after this experience, and because I honestly believe that he will use this situation for good, as it says in Romans 8:28

> . . . we know that in all things God works for the good of those who love him, who have been called according to his purpose.

I had always believed that 'praising through our circumstances' had meant that we had to wipe our tears, jump up and down with our hands in the air, carefree, praising God . . . but I was wrong. We can praise God when we have tears streaming down our faces, and mascara running everywhere. We can praise God when we are doubtful and uncertain and when we are desperate, because God is God and we should praise him simply for that. God meets us where we are, whether our lives are going the way we want them to, or not, or when our closest friend is raped and we don't know how we can stand to live in the same city as her attacker for the next three years of our lives. It doesn't matter how we come before God with praise. The important thing is that we do indeed praise him, for all that he has done, is doing and for all that he will do in using all kinds of situations and circumstances.

We can praise God when we have tears streaming down our faces, and mascara running everywhere.

WHEN THE TEARS FALL[9]

I've had questions without answers
I've known sorrow, I have known pain.
But there's one thing that I cling to
You are faithful, Jesus You're true

When hope is lost
I call You Saviour
When pain surrounds
I call You Healer
When silence falls
You'll be the song within my heart

In the lone hour of my sorrow,
Through the darkest night of my soul,
You surround me, You sustain me,
My defender for ever more

When hope is lost
I call You Saviour
When pain surrounds
I call You Healer
When silence falls
You'll be the song within my heart

And I will praise You
I will praise You
When the tears fall
Still I will sing to You
I will praise You
Jesus I will praise You
Through the suffering
Still I will sing to You

When hope is lost
I call You Saviour,
When pain surrounds
I call You Healer
When silence falls
You'll be the song within my heart

I will praise You
I will praise You
When the tears fall
Still I will sing to You
I will praise You
Jesus I will praise You
Through the suffering
Still I will sing to You

When the laughter fails to comfort
When my heart aches, Lord You'll be there
When confusion is all around me
And the darkness is my closest friend.
Still I'll praise You,
Jesus praise You

GOD IS STILL GOD – OUR TERMS VERSUS HIS

Why is God only God on our terms? The more I think about it, the more I realize that the majority of the time, for us, God is only God when we decide that he is – on our terms. Why is it that when we feel like it, God is just fabulous, we love him more than words can tell, and we want to praise him forever, but at other times we question his plans, maybe even his existence or, worse still, not even consider him at all? It's easy to proclaim God as Saviour when all is going well, but when things go badly it's not so easy to acknowledge him. In my experience, if God were only God on my terms he wouldn't be God a lot of the time.

Why is God such a disposable part of our lives?

Why is God such a disposable part of our lives? Like me, most people will have had friends who made them feel used. These so-called friends only spend time with you when they want a favour, and will dispose of you the moment you've helped them out. It's not a nice feeling and I try my very best not to be this kind of friend. We are all guilty to a certain extent of taking people for granted but I'd like to think that none of the people in my life feel continually and relentlessly used by me. But do we ever think about the way in which we treat God?

There is nothing that we could do to make God love us any more or any less and yet we repeatedly use him, regardless of the fact that we do not like to be used ourselves and know how awful it feels. God is still God regardless of who we are, what we've done, what has happened or how we feel. So why would our own lives dictate the status of God? We say we can't see God in the situation and that we can't feel his presence or hear his voice. Do we ever stop to think that we might not be looking hard enough? Why should God do all the running? Do we even want to see him? Often we may be afraid of letting God in because that means accepting that we can't control everything in our lives. Letting go of something and leaving it in God's hands can be very difficult to do.

A while ago, I was in a morning meeting at a well-known conference and the speaker talked about faith and about God still being God, regardless of anything. He handed out pieces of paper and asked us to think and pray about a situation that we were finding hard to deal with and hand over to God. He wanted us to write down the situation or problem on the piece of paper and ending our sentence with: 'You're still God and I know that you're still here'.

'You're still God and I know that you're still here'.

At the time, I had gone only six weeks without cutting myself, had been promised therapy but didn't know whether I would actually receive any and didn't know what was going to happen. I don't really know how seriously I took the talk that day because I was so self-involved with the situation but this is what I wrote: 'Even if the therapy doesn't work out – you're still God and I know that you're still here'.

I have not cut myself, or even had an urge to, since that day, six weeks before the conference. The therapy I was promised never came and I had to get help another way, but God was still God and still is.

I want to encourage you to write your own 'You're still God' statements, to slowly hand over the situations and circumstances you find yourself in to God, and to have faith in him and his deliverance. I'm not saying that by writing something down on a piece of paper your problems are going to be quickly and simply resolved. But from my experience, that simple task of pinpointing the issue and handing it over to God with faith and trust is enough to remind you time and time again that God is continually with you, at your side, his hand on your shoulder. No matter what's going on, God is a steady hope, a solid rock in the face of uncertainty and doubt. It helped me greatly to hand the situation over to God and to accept his help. Despite all the support I'd had, and everything I'd done to try to help myself, until I wrote down my 'You're still God' statement, I had not wholly and entirely handed over the situation to him and let go of the reins that I'd held on to for so long. But when I did, God was in control and it was from that moment that my recovery truly began.

No matter what's going on, God is a steady hope.

THE IMPORTANCE OF TALKING THERAPIES

As humans, we think that we can handle anything and stand up to everything that the world throws at us. We don't react well to criticism and don't like admitting failure. We are proud creatures and often prefer to put on a brave face rather than ask for help.

But sometimes we need to admit defeat. We can't always deal with everything that is thrown at us. But that doesn't make us failures. How can we possibly do everything? We're only human, after all.

We need to accept the help that is available to us. There are people out there who are trained to help us; the sole purpose of their employment is to teach people to deal with their issues, whatever they may be, so that they may be free from them. It's what these professionals are there for.

We need to accept the help that is available to us.

Some of us may feel that we are failures because we're unable to deal with our own problems, and that by admitting this weakness we are letting ourselves and our loved ones down. But actually, admitting that you cannot cope alone is one of the most courageous things that anyone can do. Acknowledging that there is a problem that you cannot solve alone and actively doing something about it is a step towards fixing it. It is well worth any shame or embarrassment you might feel in admitting it.

Admitting I needed help *was* one of the hardest things I have ever done, but I would do it all again if necessary, without hesitation. To obtain a full recovery, some kind of therapy is essential. Talking therapy treats the underlying causes of a problem, unlike drug therapy which usually just suppresses the symptoms. It is possible to achieve a certain amount of recovery without professional help, sometimes even a significant amount. But we are not meant to deal with everything on our own, and although friends and family can be an enormous support, they are often too emotionally involved in the situation.

A therapist or counsellor will be rational, will give you honest opinions and will have no emotional attachment to you. They are trained and know exactly what they are talking about. Yours will not be the first case they will have seen. Talking to a stranger about personal thoughts and feelings can sound very daunting, but I found talking to a therapist easier than talking to someone I knew. There are no connections, and they won't be even slightly shocked by what you are telling them. He or she will be someone that you will most likely never see again. They are not there to judge you; they are simply there to help you in a professional capacity.

They are not there to judge you; they are simply there to help you in a professional capacity.

Build up the courage to accept assistance. Speak to your doctor who can refer you or, if you are still in school or college, speak to a teacher that you trust. Most schools have their own child psychologist, and these people are employed for your benefit. All you need to do is overcome a little pride and simply ask.

THE POWER OF PRAYER

I tell you the truth, if anyone says to this mountain, 'Go, throw yourself into the sea,' and does not doubt in his heart but believes that what he says will happen, it will be done for him. Therefore I tell you, whatever you ask for in prayer, believe that you have received it, and it will be yours (Mk. 11:23,24).

Prayer means being able to have a conversation with the most powerful being there ever has been, and ever will be. James 5:13–19 states that prayer is a fundamental part of our spiritual lives. We don't all need to be intercessors but we are all called to pray; it's not just an activity for the 'super-holy'. Prayer is an ordinary thing. We find God in normal, everyday life. God wants to weave himself into our daily routine. It can be so easy to put prayer off, so it's far better to take five minutes now rather than saying, 'I'll do it later.'

Prayer means being able to have a conversation with the most powerful being there ever has been, and ever will be.

We often ask God for help in times of trouble and God delights in us asking, which is wonderful. God doesn't listen to us on the basis of what *we've* done or who *we* are, he listens to us on the basis of who *he* is and what *Jesus* has done for us. But we also need to tune into God and pray the things on his heart. We sometimes pray only about what's bothering us and forget to listen to God. Although God loves hearing what's going on with us at the moment, he doesn't want us to ignore his feelings either. It would be like calling a friend for a chat, not even asking how he or she was, but just diving straight into what our problems were, talking non-stop for an hour, and then saying,

'Actually, I don't have time to ask how you are. Bye.' Praying is like a conversation with a friend; we need to remember to listen as well as talking!

Praying is like a conversation with a friend; we need to remember to listen as well as talking!

Forgiveness is a condition for having our prayers answered. We often expect God to answer our prayers when we have not come before him to confess our own sins. We need to put our faith and trust in him.

- We need to confess our sins to God.
- We need to move away from habits of doubting.
- We need to obey the Holy Spirit immediately.
- We need to acknowledge Jesus as our Lord constantly.

Some ideas for creative prayer

Candles

Use candles to represent a person or situation that you want to hold up to God in prayer.

Stones

Hold a stone in your hand symbolizing something that you want to bring before God. In your own time, let the stone drop into a bucket of water, representing that you have handed it over to him.

Paper

In your own time, write down a name or situation you want to bring before God and, when you are ready, burn that piece of paper or throw it away, signifying that it is now in God's hands.

HOW DO WE MEASURE OUR WORTH?

How do you measure your worth? By your performance in school, university or at work? By the designer labels on the clothes you wear? By where you live or by how much money you or your family earn? Maybe by the people you socialize with? Do you constantly worry about being popular, and being accepted and loved by other people?

Do you constantly worry about being popular, and being accepted and loved by other people?

An earlier chapter talked about how we are surrounded by advertising that constantly makes us feel that we don't measure up. Magazines, television and newspapers tell us that we should look a certain way, use a certain product, gain or lose weight, change our partner and improve our sex lives, along with many other life-enhancing suggestions that will supposedly boost our worth in worldly values.

I've been very prone to questioning my worth over the last few years. I have a hugely competitive streak in me, but rather than just a bit of healthy competition, I became obsessed with being the best at everything I did. I would measure my worth by so many different things, but here are my top five

- school achievements
- the way I looked when I got up/during the day/when I went out/when I went to bed
- how many friends I had
- the attention I received from boys
- whether or not I was cutting myself

I cared more about whether I'd met my own high standards than I did about what other people thought of me. Although other people's negative comments hurt, it is far easier to brush them off when you are happy with yourself. In any case, I had more than enough problems trying to live up to my own unrealistically high expectations.

> **If I saw someone who was thinner or prettier than me, I'd hate myself.**

Naturally, it was very hard to always be the best at everything and if someone did better than me in an exam I would wonder why I'd done so badly. If I saw someone who was thinner or prettier than me, I'd hate myself, and if a friend was cruel to me I would blame myself, regardless of whose fault it was. If one of my friends received more attention from a guy than I did, then I would wonder what was wrong with me and then come to the conclusion that it was because I was ugly and fat. Most of these situations led to cutting myself which would be the beginning of a vicious circle: I would cut myself, feel guilty about it, which in turn made me feel like a failure, so I'd despise myself and that would make me cut myself, and the whole thing would start again.

I can clearly remember the first time someone told me that I was in the middle of a vicious circle and that I had to break it. The key is to eliminate one of the factors, because without that factor the circle cannot continue. For me the main factor I needed to eliminate was the failure, as it had always been one of my biggest issues, and everything that I felt about myself stemmed from my feelings of failure. Obviously I couldn't stop feeling this way overnight; I had to train myself out of bad ways of thinking about myself. I won't pretend it was easy, and I still have days where I'm not too keen on myself, but I've slowly learnt to be realistic and rational and to try and see things from God's perspective.

Self-worth is such a big thing in our daily lives and in our culture. Many of my friends also continually question their worth. Two of my close friends are dangerously bulimic – one of them since the age of fourteen. I've got friends who sleep around and ones who've regularly had to take morning-after pills due to unprotected sex. When we were seventeen I supported one of my closest friends through a horrific abortion, although it went against my own personal beliefs. I've got friends who've dabbled with self-harm and those who drink excessive amounts of alcohol. I know so many people who dislike and even hate themselves, and I don't think I know one person who doesn't have their own insecurities.

> **I know so many people who dislike and even hate themselves.**

Say I stood in front of you with a £10 note in my hands. What's it worth? Ten pounds in sterling British currency, right? So what if I rip it in half? Sure, it's in two pieces now, but if I was to ask you what it is, it's still a £10 note; it's still worth ten pounds regardless of the condition that it is in. Well, we can relate that to how God sees us. My life certainly can't be compared to a crisp £10 note. At times I've felt that everything I am has been so systematically damaged and destroyed and ripped into so many pieces that I can never be whole again. So often, our lives are not what God planned for us. Luckily for us though, our worth in God's eyes does not change, he does not criticize or measure us against each other. In God's eyes, we are still the original crisp £10 note. Often when we compare ourselves unfavourably to others, we feel that we have nothing to contribute. But what does God's book have to say about worth?

Now the body [of Christ] is not made up of one part but of many. If the foot should say, 'Because I am not a hand, I do not belong to the body,' it would not for that reason cease to be part of the body. . . . If the whole body were an eye, where would the sense of hearing be? . . . But in fact God has arranged the parts in the body, every one of them, just as he wanted them to be. . . . those parts of the body that seem to be weaker are indispensable . . .
(See 1 Cor. 12:14–18,22)

This is such an important passage, as it not only teaches us about how we are all an integral part of God's plan, but also shows us why we shouldn't compare ourselves to each other. If everyone had the same talents and did the same job, 'the body' wouldn't work. But God blessed us with different talents and gifts and we all have a place in his work and his plan. So instead of comparing ourselves to each other, we can trust that God has an awesome plan for our lives and that he will equip us with the tools that we will need.

But God blessed us with different talents and gifts.

['']For I know the plans I have for you,' declares the LORD, *'plans to prosper you and not to harm you, plans to give you hope and a future['']* (Jer. 29:11).

GETTING GOD'S PERSPECTIVE

As I've said before, failure has always been a big issue for me. I think everyone probably feels like a failure at some point. Maybe not to the extent of self-hate, but I'm sure that we've all felt the familiar pang of 'I wish I'd done better'. Parents sometimes feel like they have failed as parents, even when something happens to their child that was out of their control. As students in school or university, we are continually pushed to our limits to get the best grades that we possibly can and fulfil our potential. When we don't achieve what we were supposed to, we feel like we've let ourselves and other people down.

When we don't achieve what we were supposed to, we feel like we've let ourselves and other people down.

We often hear about athletes taking illegal, performance-enhancing drugs, and the market for products that promise amazing results – younger-looking skin, more energy, more pleasure, improved concentration and so on – is booming.

How do we feel when these products don't live up to our expectations? Cheated? Lied to? Conned? How do we feel when we don't reach the standards that we set for ourselves? Useless? That we've failed ourselves and others? Even worthless, maybe? The world's perspective is a harsh one. It teaches us to want to improve ourselves in this way or that way, but for all the wrong reasons.

There is nothing wrong with setting targets; we all need something to work towards. Without aspirations, we wouldn't have anything to look forward to. Without goals we can become complacent, and maybe even lazy. If we've got a specific job that we need to do then it's a good idea to plan what we are going to do and then give ourselves a reasonable target. Did you notice I just used the word 'reasonable'? I could also have said 'achievable', 'sensible' or 'realistic'. If you had just begun to build a house from scratch, and decided that you wanted to give yourself a target, for example: the date you wanted to move in to the completed house, you wouldn't make that date next week, would you? Of course, some sensible targets are easier to set than others, but we must try to be rational, to know our own strengths as well as our weaknesses and to be realistic with our goals.

> **I did incredibly well in my exams, but I didn't quite attain the goal that I had set myself.**

As a teenager, I set myself the very unrealistic goal of achieving straight A*s in my 13 GCSEs, and although I did incredibly well in my exams, I didn't quite attain the goal that I had set myself, and because of that I caused myself a lot of physical and emotional pain. I felt as if I had not only let myself down, but also my family and my teachers. I did exactly the same thing with other exams. My relationships, talents and gifts came under the same harsh scrutiny until my life became quite literally one big unachievable goal.

Let's take a look at what God has to say. What do these verses from the Bible tell us about feeling like failures and how can we apply them to our lives?

> . . . *my unfailing love for you will not be shaken nor my covenant of peace be removed* . . . (Is. 54:10).

God is telling us that his love for us will never change – there is nothing we can do that will make him love us any more or any less than he always has done – and that the peace that he brings will never be taken away from us either. In the context of failure, this verse can tell us that although we may feel like we have failed ourselves, failed others and maybe even that we have failed God himself, he does not look upon us as failures, we are still his children and he still loves us unconditionally. Sometimes we need to take a deep breath, stand back, take a long hard look at the situation, and ask ourselves why we feel as if we have failed and why it is so important to us. If God is not forcing us to achieve straight A*s then why are we doing that to ourselves? We need to try and see the situation from God's perspective.

> . . . I do not even judge myself . . . It is the Lord who judges me. Therefore judge nothing before the appointed time; wait till the Lord comes. He will bring to light what is hidden in darkness and will expose the motives of men's hearts. At that time each will receive his praise from God (1 Cor. 4:3–5).

In this extract, Paul is writing to the people of Corinth and explaining that it is God who judges him and no one else – not even Paul himself. This is true for us also; so why do we judge ourselves? We need to gain God's perspective and to learn to be a little less harsh on ourselves. God is the only one who has the right to judge us and we need to remember that and to stop ourselves when we feel like we are being self-critical and hard on ourselves and each other.

God is the only one who has the right to judge us.

> . . . stand firm. Let nothing move you. Always give yourselves fully to the work of the Lord, because you know that your labour in the Lord is not in vain (1 Cor. 15:58).

Paul writes that we need to apply ourselves to God's work and focus less on ourselves. Sometimes when we work towards our own personal gain, our goals are unachievable and when we don't meet them we feel like failures. But by giving our all to God and to his work, our efforts will not be wasted.

ACCOUNTABILITY

Being accountable simply means having someone to whom you are answerable for your actions. They should be someone with whom you can share what you're going through and who can advise and encourage you.

And we urge you . . . encourage the timid, help the weak . . . (1 Thes. 5:14).

Having self-harmed for more than two years of my life, I can give no better advice than to be accountable to somebody as soon as possible. I was so blessed to have an incredible group of friends who supported me through everything and whose never-ending love and patience will stick with me forever. But sometimes it is better to be accountable to someone older and wiser. Often your friends may be going through a lot of the same things as you, or they may have other problems of their own; something as serious as self-harm places a lot of pressure and responsibility on them.

I was so blessed to have an incredible group of friends who supported me.

For this reason, I'd wholeheartedly recommend someone a little older, a little wiser, slightly more removed from the situation. Someone who could potentially have far more insight as they are not as close to you as other friends may be. It's so important to talk about how you feel, and they will be able to listen. Although it seems like a great place to be, denial isn't progressive and won't help you in any way. Once you can admit that you have a problem that needs to be sorted, the hardest part is over. Habitual self-harm can sometimes become almost 'part of you', and by giving it up you may feel that part of your being will be taken away. Sometimes you don't want to see your scars fade because you're worried that you won't know who you are any more or how you will function.

> **Having someone to be accountable to can help you see and think rationally.**

Having someone to be accountable to can help you see and think rationally. Having all your thoughts locked up inside your head slowly makes the problem worse, and you are far more likely to become irrational if you only have your own feelings and opinions to go by. The person doesn't have to be a Christian, though of course a Christian mentor is even better as they can pray with you, and bring a spiritual element into the equation.

I was lucky enough to have three people that I was accountable to in different degrees. All three were caring, wise and at least fifteen years older than me. They were not connected in any way and don't know each other.

The first was a friend I love so dearly. I've known her for what seems like my whole life. She's a mature Christian who was always there for me, regardless of anything. She is someone who, over the years, would not only talk things through with me, but who would also pray with me and for me, which is one of the important things anyone could do for a friend.

The second was a teacher who taught me while I was at school. She was genuinely concerned for my well-being, and started things moving to help me get better. She would spend time with me when I was at my most distressed – at school. Although she was not someone who would pray with me, her commitment was astonishing, and although having to admit my harmful behaviour to her was extremely difficult, the outcome was amazing; she helped me regain my self-esteem and confidence and taught me some of my most important lessons in life.

The last is a friend who I don't get the chance to see as much of as I'd like to. She is also someone who especially over the last year or so has just been there for me, without any hype or drama. She would just sit and talk and pray with me, and although I only see her a few times a year, she too encouraged me, and was committed to looking out for my welfare.

I've mentioned these people because they were exactly what I needed to help me recover. They have families of their own, they have their own lives, but they were still willing to help me through my difficulties. You will probably know and trust people who you think have too much to deal with themselves to have time for your problems. They too may have their own families, their own lives, but once they know how you feel, they will support you, because they will want to see you get the help you need. These people will want to be there for you, but you need to give them the chance to do this. They're people who will stand by you and help you through difficult times, and bring you out the other side.

Once they know how you feel, they will support you.

These people can encourage your progress. You will need someone who will tell you that you're doing well having gone eight months without cutting and then slipping up. Someone who will tell you that next time it could be a year – someone who will help you to restore your faith in yourself. These people are invaluable, but remember too that they don't have all the answers. Unless they've been there themselves, they won't be able to understand totally, so don't be disappointed if sometimes they don't seem to have the answer to every question you have.

I still have mentors to a certain degree, and I am most definitely still accountable to people regardless of the fact that I no longer self-harm. I'm not talking about people I see every day or even every week, but people I can be completely truthful with, and who I know will be honest with me. People I can catch up with and talk to, share my troubles with, talk through situations with, who just encourage me to keep on going. These are some of the people that I have the most respect and love for, because of the way in which they've cared for me and enabled me to help myself. Being accountable to someone will be one of the most important things you will ever do on your journey to recovery.

ALTERNATIVE COPING MECHANISMS

Sometimes it can feel impossible to abstain from cutting. At times like these we become hysterical and irrational and can't see beyond our feelings. All logic leaves us and at those times we feel that we need to cut ourselves because we think that nothing else will do. Sadly, the feeling of relief that we experience from having let out our pain and anxiety by cutting does not last for long.

If you can abstain from just one cut, you can then break the circle.

That feeling of relief is very quickly replaced by feelings of guilt, regret and more desperation. The circle is a vicious one and needs to be broken. If you can abstain from just one cut, you can then break the circle and put some different coping mechanisms into place. There are many different coping mechanisms that will provide a similar feeling of relief. Below are just some that have been particularly useful to me.

Write down your feelings

Writing things down can help release those feelings. Write a diary, a poem or a song. These can clarify things and help you make sense of your thoughts. It is a very therapeutic exercise and is an extremely useful distraction. Even if you don't think you can write full sentences, just jot down words. If you are artistic, try painting or drawing something representative of how you feel: the main thing is to be honest about what you're feeling right here and now, even if it's painful to do so.

Imagine your favourite place

Breathe deeply and imagine a place where you've been at your most happy, or even an imaginary place where you would love to be. Keep that image in your mind and concentrate upon it, trying to put in as much detail as you can. Do this until you are feeling calmer and the feelings of wanting to harm yourself have passed.

Have ice at hand

This strategy works well because although you may feel some kind of pain, you are not damaging yourself in any way. All you need to do is hold some ice in your hands. After a while, holding the ice will become painful. Do this until your harmful feelings have passed.

Elastic bands

Like the ice exercise, this strategy works by making you feel like you are self-harming. Simply let the elastic snap against your body. This can be painful but won't damage you. Once again, do this until the urge to cut has gone.

Felt-tip pens

Use a red felt-tip pen to draw on the part of your body where you feel like you need to cut. By doing this you will see what looks like cuts but you won't be hurting yourself.

Here are some suggestions for things to do to help deal with anger or frustration, without hurting yourself

- Biting on something like a lemon to give you a sharp sensation.
- Talking to someone.
- Hitting something not alive, such as a pillow or punch-bag.
- Squeezing putty and then stretching it until it snaps.

- Listening to loud or angry music and singing or dancing along.
- Throwing ice against a wall so it shatters, or hitting a tree with a stick.

If you suffer from low self-esteem then the following suggestions may be useful

- Pampering yourself: having a bath, listening to soothing music, burning incense, watching television or reading, getting a haircut, going shopping – anything that makes you feel taken care of or comforted.
- Phoning or visiting a friend.
- Listing the good things about yourself.
- Soothing body lotion on the areas you want to harm.
- Crying.
- Thinking of not harming as a form of punishment if you feel you need to be punished.

It is important to understand that although these coping mechanisms are available to give you an alternative to harming yourself at times of desperation, it is very unlikely that these strategies will completely prevent you from self-harming, and they do not solve the main problem. At this point, it is crucial to state that these are most definitely not substitutes for professional help of any kind. In order to make a full recovery, professional guidance really is a necessity.

A note to family and friends

The road to recovery will be hard and possibly very long for your loved one. Certain coping mechanisms mentioned above may seem inappropriate as they may cause a certain amount of discomfort, such as the use of ice or elastic bands. It must be stressed that these are not intended for long-term use. They may prevent the self-harmer from causing permanent damage to him or herself, but they are not intended to be used in the place of professional help. Professional help will be the key to recovery.

The road to recovery will be hard and possibly very long.

I LOVE MY FRIEND BUT I FEEL POWERLESS TO HELP

We are only responsible for ourselves and for our own actions. We can advise, encourage and be there for our loved ones, but at the end of the day we cannot make their decisions for them or control their actions. Everyone is responsible for their own actions.

It can be extremely hard when we see someone we love going through pain and we feel so powerless because we feel we can't help them in any way. However, while we cannot take away their pain, we are not totally powerless.

We don't have to be a trained psychologist in order to be supportive. We can be there to listen during times of need, and we can be a shoulder to cry on. We can advise if necessary and encourage the person to seek professional help. We can simply let them know that we are there for them at any time, and love them for who they are, regardless of their problems.

It can be extremely hard when we see someone we love going through pain.

I've been in both situations. I've been the friend supporting a self-harmer through their pain, so I know how difficult it can be to know what to say and do. You want to tell them that it will all be fine and that they'll soon feel better but you can't tell them when or how.

I've also been on the receiving end of love and support. And although it may seem to you at the time that your words are useless and your support isn't enough, to the person you're supporting it means the world. Just to know that someone cares can get you through the day. You may not be able to cure your friend, but simply being there for them means a lot.

When I found out that someone I loved had begun self-harming I felt very responsible. I felt that because I had self-harmed, I had somehow given my friend the same idea. But we are all responsible for our own actions. My friend may have turned to self-harm even if I hadn't myself, particularly as self-harm affects so many young people now. If you are in the same situation, be assured that you are not responsible for your friend's actions. They themselves have decided to take that route and when it comes down to it, it makes no difference whether they know another self-harmer or not. It is their mind, their life and their decision.

When I found out that someone I loved had begun self-harming I felt very responsible.

YOU ARE NOT ALONE

One of the hardest things during my period of self-harming was the feeling that I was alone in what I was going through. Not because I didn't have plenty of friends, but because I thought that I was the only person in the world who felt like this, and that there was no one out there who would understand.

Although rationally I knew that many other people suffered from self-harm, I really did feel like there wasn't anyone who could help me and who truly understood me and what I was going through. The truth is that although everyone is different, it is probably safe to say that at any given moment there are many other people in a similar situation to yours. This does not diminish the seriousness of your experience; it simply goes to show that you are not alone.

I really did feel like there wasn't anyone who could help me.

While you may be going through a terrible time, and you may not be surrounded by a supportive family and friends, there is one person that is there for you regardless of anything. He doesn't have a time schedule, and you don't need to make an appointment three weeks in advance; with him it's an open house all day, every day and he's always in. He knitted you together in your mother's womb and knows the exact number of hairs on your head. That person is Jesus. He wants to be with you through your troubles as well as your best times. He wants you to lean on his shoulder and to place your trust in him. He wants to be there for you and to gather you under his wing. His answer will always be '*Yes!*' so all that's left for you to do is ask.

Richard's Story

I first attempted self-harm when I was twelve. It began with tiny cuts made with very small blades, such as those found in pencil sharpeners and razors, and over the years developed into much more serious episodes of cutting with much larger blades, the largest of which was a 15-inch carving knife that created some of the biggest and boldest scars I'm left with today. In truth, I can't quite remember how and why it all began (copious amounts of hard drugs have a habit of impairing a person's memory!) but I'm sure that years of bullying, a few school moves and generally feeling like I didn't 'fit in' had something to do with it.

In high school I began smoking cannabis.

In high school I began smoking cannabis. Smoking cannabis led to taking stronger drugs like amphetamine and ecstasy and eventually led to cocaine and crack cocaine use in my early twenties. With the introduction of narcotics during my school years also came an increasing intensity to my self-harming. This created more bullying and unsettledness that was met with more drugs and more self-harm. Thus the vicious circle began, one that would take a few years and the authority of Jesus Christ to break.

I was admitted to a child psychiatric unit for a short time at the age of fourteen. My parents were getting desperate as my self-harming was increasing in severity. I have an uncle who at the time lived in America and was part of a Christian youth ministry there. He suggested that my father and I take a trip over and, since we had nothing to lose (neither my parents nor myself were Christians), we went. The trip lasted about a month and involved a few personal and spiritual battles. My father was saved during the trip and I had my first experience of Jesus. For six months my life was transformed. Unfortunately, before long, with the aid of a rebellious spirit, I was knee-deep in drugs and self-harm again.

At sixteen I was sectioned to an adult psychiatric ward for a few weeks.

At sixteen I was sectioned to an adult psychiatric ward for a few weeks as a result of an episode of self-harm that took a handful of police in full riot gear to subdue. After being released I was given a council flat and enough money from the government to just about survive. I began attending a local church and, after a short spell following Jesus, decided to go my own way yet again. The next few years, between the age of eighteen and twenty-one, were the most destructive of my life; full of more drugs, more self-harm and a few weeks in hospital after contracting septicaemia in an infected cut, which nearly cost me my life.

Around my twenty-first birthday, I began praying for my girlfriend at the time, who had been a heroin addict for a few years. I would pray to God that he would release her from her addiction. It was a desperate situation and I didn't know who else to turn to. Although that prayer wasn't answered, it was the catalyst for me coming to faith in Jesus.

After a few relationship issues, we split and I was left homeless. With no other options, I returned home to a family that was by now strong in faith in Jesus. I walked into a church in Cardiff, my new home, and sat unassumingly at the back. Before long I was sobbing my heart out as God forgave me for all the depraved things I had done in my past. The love of Christ came over me and from then on I felt accepted and truly loved. That was two years ago now and, to the glory of God, my life has been completely turned around. I now don't rely on any other coping mechanism except for Jesus Christ. I no longer self-harm or take drugs, I have a stable job and I'm once again considered part of society. God is beginning to use my scars, my testimony and my newly acquired heart for youth for amazing things. These are exciting times!

> God is beginning to use my scars, my testimony and my newly acquired heart for youth for amazing things.

Life after self-harm

Like Richard, I too found that there is life after self-harm. Through a combination of therapy, the love and support of my family and friends, and the healing power of Jesus my ordeal is finally over. Habitual self-harm is now becoming more and more of a distant memory every day. Sometimes I sit and think about it and I can't quite believe the point of desperation I reached. I can't ever imagine causing myself any harm now. I feel like a different person. I've gone from the girl whose whole life was 'a failure to the world and its whole existence' to someone who can accept herself for who she is – my talents as well as the things I can't do. And, after years of self-loathing, I can tell you it's an amazing feeling. I now know that I am not a failure; my self-harm was my coping strategy for the problems I couldn't deal with, but not being able to deal with those things does not make me a failure. I'm not a failure, because I have achieved so much over the years. I have been blessed with talents by God and I intend to use them. I am only human and my work really doesn't have to be perfect. I can now give myself realistic and sensible objectives and, even if I don't reach them, I've learnt to be rational (well, I'm trying at least!). I can't find the words to explain how incredible it feels to be able to write these words and actually mean them.

This may be a very strange thing to say, but I sincerely do not regret what I went through. It has made me a stronger person, it has strengthened my faith in God and I am now able to appreciate life and its fragility far more. Through my experiences I've been able to help other self-harmers through their troubles. I believe I went through this for a reason and that reason may be 2 Corinthians 1:3,4, which says

Praise be to the God and Father of our Lord Jesus Christ, the Father of compassion and the God of all comfort, who comforts us in all our troubles, so that we can comfort those in any trouble with the comfort we ourselves have received from God.

I have been blessed with talents by God and I intend to use them.

All I know is that it was not in vain, and that my experience will not be lost or wasted. Richard and I are living proof that it is possible to recover from self-harm. All it takes is the desire to get better, the determination to do something about it before it's too late and the willpower to see it through. Yes, the road may be long and hard, but the prize at the end of it will be worth more than anything in the world. And that's the honest truth – from someone who's been there, done that and got the scars, but who's wearing a smile.

The plans I have for you
(Based on Jeremiah 29:11)

Feeling lost, feeling frightened,
Running without knowing my destination
With eyes wide shut and only selective hearing
Moving forward but continually looking back.
Feeling faint, feeling desperate,
My relevance hits ground zero
Ignorance seems a beautiful path to take
I can't see the garden for the weeds . . .

But then a voice, the same unchanging voice:
'You will prosper, you won't be harmed
Come to me, talk to me – I promise I'll listen
Let your heart find me, you'll find me, you'll find me.
I'll save you and bring you back
These are the plans I have for you.'

Feeling worthless, feeling sick
I can't go on like this anymore.
Denial offers a promising olive branch.
At least for now I can pretend I'm OK.
Feeling finished, feeling done
So young and yet at the point of no return.
Memory sticks in a painful knife
A reminder of why I'm here at all . . .

But then a voice, the same unchanging voice:
'You will prosper, you won't be harmed
Come to me, talk to me – I promise I'll listen
Let your heart find me, you'll find me, you'll find me.
I'll save you and bring you back
These are the plans I have for you.'

Feeling better, feeling loved
Though the process is long and hard,
Step by step a little further each day
Determination never let me go,
Feeling grateful, feeling free
Desperation a memory I'd prefer to forget.
Realization kicks in – I know that I'm lucky
A word I'd never have used before . . .

But then a voice, the same unchanging voice:
'You have prospered, you were not harmed
You came to me, you talked to me – I told you I'd listen
Your heart found me, you found me, you found me.
I saved you and brought you back
These are the plans I had for you.'

I'll never let you go.

WANT TO KNOW MORE?

So maybe you've read this book and want to know more about Christianity, and what it means to be a Christian. The Alpha Course is a long-standing course run at hundreds of churches. It aims to help you to find the meaning of life and deals with any questions that you may have. Details can be found on the Alpha Course website {http://alpha.org/uk/}.

Maybe you would like to ask Jesus Christ to come and be Lord of your life. If that's you, have a look at these Bible verses

> *I am the way and the truth and the life. No-one comes to the Father except through me (Jn. 14:6).*

> *For God so loved the world that he gave his one and only Son, that whoever believes in him shall not perish but have eternal life (Jn. 3:16).*

> *. . . everyone who believes in him receives forgiveness of sins through his name (Acts 10:43).*

If you believe that these words from the Bible are God's personal promises to you, then you can respond in three simple steps

1 *Sorry* – We all need to repent. This means that we simply need to ask God to forgive us for all the things that we have done wrong in our lives.

2 *Thank you* – We need to thank Jesus for dying on the cross for us so that we can be forgiven.

3 *Please* – No one can force us to believe in God and God himself will not force us to either. We need to invite him to come into our lives and to fill us with his Holy Spirit.

If you would like to be able to have a personal relationship with Jesus Christ, then here is a simple prayer

Lord Jesus,
I know that I have done wrong in my life and I am truly sorry. Please forgive me now as I turn from everything which I know is wrong. Thank you so much for dying on the cross so that I could be set free from my sins. I ask you please to come into my life, and that you would continually fill me up with your Holy Spirit. Amen.

USEFUL CONTACT INFORMATION

www.selfharmuk.org

www.nshn.co.uk (National Self Harm Network)

www.youngminds.org.uk/selfharm

Emergency Services
Telephone: 999

ChildLine
Freepost 1111, London N1 0BR
Freephone 0800 1111

The Samaritans
Telephone: 08457 90 90 90
Website: www.samaritans.org.uk
Email: jo@samaritans.org

National Health Service (NHS)
Telephone: 0845 46 47
Website: www.nhsdirect.nhs.uk

Rape Crisis Centre
Website: www.rapecrisis.org.uk

Alcoholics Anonymous
Telephone: 0845 769 7555
Website: www.alcoholics-anonymous.org.uk

Release (National drugs and legal helpline)
Telephone: 0845 4500 215

FURTHER READING

Burns, D.D., *The Feeling Good Handbook* (New York: Plume, 1989).

Fennell, M., *Overcoming Low Self-Esteem* (London: Constable and Robinson, 1999).

Schmidt, U. and K. Davidson, *Life After Self-Harm: A Guide to the Future* (Oxford: Routledge, 2004).

END NOTES

1 Mental Health Self-Harm Inquiry, www.mentalhealth.org.uk

2 http://www.samaritans.org.uk/know/pressoffice/news/2007/
news_210507.html

3 http://www.samaritans.org.uk/know/information/informationsheets/
selfharm/selfharm_sheet.shtm

4 Mind, 'Understanding Self-Harm' information booklet (revised,
2003), www.mind.org.uk

5 Samaritans, 'Self-Harm' information sheet, www.samaritans.org.uk

6 Samaritans, 'Self-Harm' information sheet, www.samaritans.org.uk

7 Samaritans, 'Self-Harm' information sheet, www.samaritans.org.uk

8 Mental Health UK, 'The Truth About Self-Harm',
www.selfharmuk.org

9 Tim Hughes, 'When the Tears Fall', *When Silence Falls* (EMI CMG:
2004)